BAN EN BANLIEUE

T0161127

Bhanu Kapil BAN EN BANLIEUE

NIGHTBOAT BOOKS, NEW YORK

Printed in the United States
Fourth Printing, 2023

ISBN: 978-1-937658-24-3

Cover photograph: Back Garden, Colorado, 2013.

Design and typesetting by Margaret Tedesco
Text set in Plantin and Futura

Cataloging-in-publication data is available
from the Library of Congress

Nightboat Books
New York
www.nightboat.org

Hayes, Middlesex, 2012.

1. [13 Errors for Ban]:

A preface. Ash. A sore.

A re-telling—tiny movements—of a scene from Ban. "The weight of my head pushing down on the floor opens my mouth," says Laura Ann. "It's not the mouth that wants to open, necessarily. It's the gravity, the pressure, the force...." As Laura Ann's mouth [jaw] opens, deep in the pose, I notice that her legs part. From behind. At that moment, I realize I have not written the part of Ban that is about sex—the bad sex of the riot. Two weeks later, exhausted, trying to write [re-write] Ban, as I do every day, I lean over to the bookshelf and brush [touch] *Dictee*, a book I have not read for many years. I close my eyes then open them, my finger on page 4. A volt of violet [orange] fire goes through my body when I read these words: "Now the weight from the uppermost back of her head, pressing downward. It stretches evenly, the entire skull expanding tightly all sides the front of her head. She gasps from its pressure, its contracting motion." In this way, Cha's "dead tongue" licks the work. No. I feel her licking me. The inside of my arm, the inside of my ear. My error. I wake up. It's time for the auto-sacrifice to begin.

2. AUTO-SACRIFICE (Notes):

Though I cannot bear it. I make a table out of the notes and smooth down its long red tail. A ribbon. That extends into the aisle. I press click and the sentences are abruptly regulated in ways a baby could have figured out. No offense to babies. No offense to chimpanzees. I think of the grid as a sanctuary, an orphanage, a home—for the sentences to be. Though at any moment I might press click again. In fact, I went to a sanctuary for chimps in Louisiana, near the border with Texas. At any time, the chimps could be removed—to a lab at Oklahoma State University—for a test. An experiment. Then returned. I went there. I pretended to be a volunteer with Jordan and JT, two MFA students from Baton Rouge. We stuffed Donkey Kongs with peanut butter and threw them over the hedge. Is this how you become a writer? It's still not real to me—what the sentences are for and how long they might go on.

3. STORIES:

No, I don't think so. I wrote a companion series or sequence of childhood stories to lie next to Ban, but when it was time to publish them, here (in section 3), I pressed the delete button and stored them in another file. "I am not interested in disclosure. I am interested in discharge," said Petra Kuppers in the café in Berkeley that served vegan chocolate cake in 2011. We were meeting for the first time. No stories of early life, or any part of life, were exchanged, in the culture I was now a part of yet distinct from my own. "I'm sorry," said Petra Kuppers, "but I'm not interested in your story. I'm not interested in where you are from."

4. END-NOTES:

Extreme gratitude to the other writers and non-writers who encouraged me to take risks in venues of all kinds. Curation worked out for me. Performance art worked out for me. It helped me to think. Is there something wrong with me? I withheld the stories now this. These notes that are not for writing but for you. For example, I didn't get to the part with Kapil Muni— a section [incarnate], regressed: a woman who—Ban-like—contorted [leaped] out of a sacrificial [bridal] fire and is [was] carried out to sea—the Bay of Bengal— on the backs of tiny pink dolphins. How her burns were sucked and fused by sea creatures: their microscopic mouths. Bronze-copper, supine—mid ocean—she's balanced on the back of a whale. Lightning strikes her body in a pagan tableau and she: opens her milky eyes. Kapil Muni—seated—opens his third-eye as she drifts past Sagar Island—and sends a beam of gold [rose] [blue] light to her. I wanted Ban to receive the energy too, simultaneously, here—but would blank out—each time—the section, the time, the body. What kind of person blanks out eternal time? It is okay. Not even in the end parts could I approach this area, the gift, a color healing so radical it extends to a future self—that was not mine.

5. BUTCHER'S BLOCK APPENDIX:

97.5% of the work of Ban happened in notebooks, public or otherwise. One day, my neighbor put her butcher's block on the curb. I got it and washed it down, stacking the notebooks in the three wire cages beneath the chopping board. I printed out the pages from my blog, where I had written Ban in a frenzy, and tucked those in as well. In this way, writing, I was able to turn from the computer to the dormant yet demonstrative materials: there. On the slab. In reality, the apparatus was not accessible; the wire cages kept getting caught. Thus, on December 21st, 2012—the winter solstice—I made an appendix, opening the notebooks at random and setting my fingertip down. My fingertip was like an "extended periphery." Cha. My fingertip was like an animal, sensing with its delicate, representative snout. This was bibliomancy. A way to make visible something that was "no longer possible to say." Cha again. Who has arrived. In the last possible minute of the book. To augur. To be here—also. With Ban.

6a. EPIGRAPHS:

"*What time is it?*
Irradiates
the ash carapace

The greenish grey
of the flesh

—adulates—

aching the crown
carried by the scarab."

—Dolores Dorantes, tr. Jen Hofer, *Sin puertas visibles.*

"The time is 6:35 p.m.   she turns her head
exactly to the left."

—Theresa Hak Kyung Cha, *Dictee.*

○○○○

Deleted epigraphs for a novel of Ban written [from 2010 to 2014] in the contemporary tradition of Indian writing in English, itself [abandoned] in turn:

"What has been banned is delivered over to its own separateness and, at the same time, consigned to the mercy of the one who abandons it—at once excluded and included, removed and at the same time captured."

—Giorgio Agamben, *The Ban and the Wolf.*

"I understand the concern of your people. But if you keep off the streets of London and behave yourselves you won't have the SPG to worry about."

—Sir David McNee, Commissioner of the Metropolitan Police Service, defending the actions of the Special Patrol Group, to a black journalist.

Even out of context, the two deleted epigraphs betray their weightlessness and make me feel a little sick. If you were here, I would make you some mint tea and turn out the sofa for a little bed. Here you are. There it is. Let's talk about it tomorrow.

Are you alive?

6b.

One thing next to another doesn't mean they touch.

7. DEDICATION:

This book is dedicated to Blair Peach, the teacher from New Zealand who protested a gathering of the National Front in the town hall of Southall, Middlesex (U.K.)—an immigrant suburb of West London—the *banlieue* of the title—on April 23rd, 1979. He is the martyr of my novel although he does not appear in it. He appears here. He appears now. He appears before the novel begins. Knocked unconscious by a member of the Metropolitan Police Special Patrol Group, Peach died the next day in Ealing Hospital. Reports acknowledging the cause of his death were made public by the Metropolitan Police on April 27th, 2010.

Blair Peach, 1979.

8. INSTALLATIONS AND PERFORMANCES:

1. Pre-Ban "butcher's shop" performance for *Both Sides and Center*, Schindler House, West Hollywood, CA, 2011.

2. Street: Lie down on sidewalk next to the ivy in the exact spot that the novel is set, somewhere between Balmoral Avenue and Lansbury Drive. Observe the sky. Install circular mirrors in the vines. Nervous system notes. Descriptions of the weather and neighborhood. Similarly, at other sites in West London, crumple aluminium foil, make a daffodil ikebana as a late April shrine. Hayes, Middlesex, England, 2012.

3. Body outline on ground ringed by candles/flowers at the site where Jyoti Singh Pandey lay for 40 minutes in December 2012, raped then thrown from the bus and gutted with a steel pipe. I walk—naked, barefoot, red—from the cinema in South Delhi where she watched the *Life of Pi*. Then caught a bus. To this spot. The anti-rape protesters make a circle around my body when I lie down. What do they receive? An image. But what happens next? How does the energy of a performance mix with the energy of the memorial? How does the image support the work that is being done in other areas? Which hormones does it produce? New Delhi, India, 2014.

4. *Poetics of Healing* "meat sack" performance. No butcher's table this time. No window. No voyeurism. No privacy. Here, I am being dragged off the stage by Jai Arun Ravine, a writer from [of] the Bay Area, in the Subterranean Arthouse at 8 p.m. The evening is part of a larger curation: "vital forms." A homeopath inverts her body, for example, to expose the surgery to her breast. Berkeley, CA, 2013.

5. Garden/mud Ban installation images, with Sharon Carlisle, earth artist and anti-fracking activist. Loveland, CO, 2012–2014.

6. *Nude page for Ban:* charcoal smudge. Esque Journal, NY, 2011.

7. Aftermath of [13 Errors for Ban]: a broad cloth stained with charcoal. Seattle, WA, 2014.

8. *Masque for Ban* with Andrea Spain, David Banash, Jamila Cornick, Emily Harrison and Emerson Fae. Naropa University Summer Writing Program. "Facism is cheap," says Andrea, when we return from Home Depot with the red gloves and glass. A "politics of sound." The rioters approach the stage. A choreography. Andrea in a gas mask smashing the glass into the steel drum with a pipe. Delicately at first. Boulder, CO, 2013.

9. *Symbolic scene for Ban.* At the last moment, it seems unbearable to read my actual writing aloud in front of a local group. Later that night, I write a brief account of the improvised performance and post it on my blog, *Was Jack Kerouac a Punjabi?:* "To strip down, partially, because nudity, to be effective, to be frightening, should be that. I read it like this—the description. Of the person who was exposed: to light. In the night-time scene. To ask three women of color, who identify as non-white in some way, to stand to my left. To ask eleven men who are white, or who identify as white, to stand to my right.... An invitation. To take, in turns, the chance to hit. Or kick. Or hit. Or hurt. The white men took in turns to hit me, then re-formed the loop. I ended the loop by saying, now the performance is over. I did not feel attenuated or vivid during the series of impacts; I felt something else." Titmouse launch. The Dikeou Collection. Denver, Colorado, 2011.

10. Performance talk on the Fearless One, social violence and Ban. Gender and Time symposium. Afterwards, I perform a wolfgirl Ban in the rose garden—face down then crawling out—for two friends. Pratt Institute, NY, 2013.

11. Collaboration with Gingger Shankar (double violin) at Mehfil Massive. It is the anniversary of the riot precisely, April 23rd. I read from *Ban*. Gingger plays *Dawn*. Los Angeles, CA, 2014.

12. Memorial ritual [street puja] for Nirbhaya on the service road parallel to the Mahipalpur Flyover, also known as the Airport Flyover. Outside Hotel 37, named in the Death Sentence judgement as the place where Nirbhaya [Jyoti Singh Pandey] was thrown from a bus after a gang rape, and where she lay for 40 minutes, her entrails black on the pink-grey street, I make a public offering. "How do you draw the ghost of the intestines?" —Laura Ann Samuelson. A group of men and boys from a nearby tobacco stand gathers to watch; my inadvertent witnesses. Curious, nervous, thin. Two men dig up a sewer next to me as I pour the red powder onto the ground. The doorman of Hotel 37 crosses the sidewalk to ask: "What kind of survey is this, madam?" Materials: sindoor (red powder) and peacock ore (a gift from CAConrad). Tonglen practice. Is this the charnel ground? Yes, it is. I collect an earth sample. I get into the taxi. The peacock ore is vibrating in my stained palm. South Delhi, India, 2014.

[13 Errors for Ban] ---

: Notes/instructions written into an AWP panel talk the night before, but also afterwards. Yes, yes. I know AWP is not cool. It is terrifying. Believe me, I spent half the conference inverted above the Puget Sound and/or drinking vodka with Maggie Z. I exaggerate. After my talk, I went to see the panel on African writers next door. A memorial for Kofi Awoonor. In the audience, I clutched my dirty sheets in a bundle to my bony chest. I wept when the time came, and left as soon as I could.

[Hold up white sheet with long red tail. Smooth it on table. Extend ribbon into aisle. Empty charcoal from Safeway plastic bag onto white sheet before talk begins. Hold up yellow sheet with black and white zig zag tail as you read the first parts of the talk.] Nude Page for Ban: "Would you, or someone else you know, smear this page with soot from a car's diesel pipe or dirt from the asphalt? And let this, this dirty page, be the page that I submit?" [Ronaldo Wilson helps me. To give the yellow sheet to the audience. He cuts his hand on the tail and bleeds all over the white sheet/charcoal mixture beneath. He makes a video. I haven't seen it yet. He shows PINK and I think: Ronaldo is the pink lightning.]

I wanted to write a novel but instead I wrote this. [Hold up charcoal in fist.] I wrote the organ sweets—the bread-rich parts of the body before it's opened then devoured. I wrote the middle of the body to its end.

This is the table. [Stroke the broad cloth.] It's an animal—"there, there."

On September 4th, 2010, at 7 p.m., I began to write—but did not write—[wrote]: Notes for a novel never written: a novel of the race riot: (Ban.) As my contribution to a panel at the limits of the poetic project—its capacity: for embodiment, for figuration, for what happens to bodies when we link them to the time of the event, which is to say—unlived time, the part of time that can never belong to us—I would like to present: a list of the errors I made as a poet engaging a novel-shaped space, the space of a book: set: on a particular day and at a particular time: April 23rd, 1979. The novel begins at 4 p.m.—just as Ban—a brown [black] girl—is walking home from school. She orients to the sound of breaking glass, and understands the coming violence has begun. Is it coming from the far-off street or is it coming from her home? Knowing that either way she's done for—she lies down to die. A novel is thus an account of a person who has already died, in advance of the death they are powerless. To prevent. "There are no angels." What will it take to shed off, to be rendered, to incarnate, to never be there in the same way again?

Error 1: [Press play on iPod so that the rest of the talk plays through the conference sound system. I don't speak for the rest of the talk. I have an idea to crush the charcoal with great force, a chunk of it in each hand. But when it's time, I can't always do what's necessary. I bring the charcoal to my mouth. I hesitate. I smash it down. I want to end the talk covered with black dust, the life food or emblem of Ban herself. Let's see what unfolds. Let's see if it's possible. To be done.]

Ban is not an immigrant; she is a shape or bodily outline that's familiar: yet inaccurate: to what the thing is. How to look good on Skype. A vaginal opening. By 2011, she's a blob of meat on the sidewalk. I progress her to meat—a monstrous form—but here she pauses, is inhibited, and this takes a long time. I make a graph of her scissoring limbs [forearms, hands, tongue] and index them to the last 12 hours: 4 p.m. to 4 a.m. [and other dominant forms]. I lie down next to her and extend my own tongue to the ivy that curls down to the sidewalk with its medicine and salt: so close to my own mouth. Lick it and you could die. I do all these things, but Ban does not die. With every rainfall, she's washed off the street but by morning, a stain rises up through the asphalt and by 4 p.m. the next day, she's ready to go again. This is the first problem of the project; an interest in duration as the force by which—something: might become. We worked on this in so many MFA classes, and yet here I am—facing the poor results of this model for Ban herself, who lies outside of time. Precisely because—as a black person or child born to immigrants in the U.K. of 1971—her birth broke something. It inserted something, like when you start to hate yourself or when you lose something. "What is born in England but is never English?" What grew a tail? What leaned over and rested its hands on its knees? An immigrant has a set of complex origins, is from elsewhere; the monster is made, on the other hand, from local mixtures of organic and inorganic materials, repurposed teeth, selenium, lungs, pink lightning, public health concerns.

2. How nudity functions in the work.

3. I thought I was writing about an immigrant. I was writing about a monster. Monsters don't incarnate. They regress.

4. Ban is a dessicating form on the sidewalk—her teeth, in contrast, are so white—turn indigo: when the headlights of oncoming cars strobe over her prone, barely visible/dark face. And hair. I should

have written the alien body as a set of fragments, a ghazal with an omega mouth and a healing cry; instead, I went with *historical fiction*—the narrative of a riot that had receded by 1983, to be overlain by other riots. The riot is a charnel ground in this sense—overlain—in the present—by concrete—poured right down—over the particular spot on the sidewalk I am speaking of—as well as—migrations—from Eastern Europe—and beyond. The causal goal for the project was to collect some of these fragments in an ultra-formal way that might not very easily, in turn, be encountered by a wide audience. I wanted the fragments to circulate then ebb, just as immigrant memory is fragile, replaced by the next incoming wave of life; little shops that stock the dried milk powder a house-wife needs for the sweet goods she makes on particular festivals and nights. And later, in Arabic, Polish, and Tamil script printed right on the glass, the words for goat, electronics, the fruit with the little black spots below the anus of the stem.

6. The project fails at every instant and you can make a book out of that and I do, in the same time that it takes other people to write their second novel that is optioned by Knopf and which details the world they grew up in, just as I am—detailing—which is to say: scouring/burnishing—the world I grew up in too.

7. What would I have written—what would have become of these materials—had I stayed in the U.K.?

8. Charcoal—the very thing Ban is made of—is so messy. I was covered from my brow to my waist like the chimney sweep in the poems of William Blake in every art class of my youth. As a teenager, I used to play truant every Wednesday and catch the train to Pimlico, still in my uniform and with my packed lunch, as if I

was going to school. I went to the Tate—every Wednesday—like clockwork—to look—at the illuminated books—of Blake—in a very dark room intended to preserve—the golden ink and peacock green or blue embellishments. The error here is that I chose to write my book in a place where these colors and memories are not readily available. There is no bank. Instead, I scream them—I scream the colors each to each—and this is difficult. It is difficult to work in simple, powerful ways with the proxy memories. For weeks at a time, I stopped writing—and when I returned, Ban was gone. She continued on without me, and what I had to do next will make you dislike me even more than you already do. I had to eat what was on the floor. I had to make an artifact out of something that had left no artifacts. I had to put the charcoal in my mouth and choke it down.

9. Although I am interested in errors, perhaps it *is* more accurate to say I wrote a book that failed—and not in the interesting vulnerable way that books sometimes fail—but in this other way—"the way of the species that isn't registered or described; that does not emerge." To replicate but not survive. At this stage of the project, I was still optimistic. Lyn Hejinian came to Naropa and gave a talk on captioning. During the Q & A, I asked: "How do you caption smoke?" She said: "You'd have to trap it first." And so I tried to trap the sounds made—sub-auditory—by Ban—in another era— but, despite my training—in Physics—to A level—I could not. Also, I was super lazy. In addition, I had suspended my normal coping mechanisms. For the better part of 2012, Ban looped—an orbital of dog shit, soot, bitumen and diesel oil—around the city. That December, energized by the solstice, I built a chrysalis in my garden. I leaned a plate of glass against the back fence. I put the glass in fiction to trap the dots and bits of Ban. But then it snowed— and the turquoise and scarlet fibers of the chrysalis poured into the

ground of my Colorado garden, where they rotted all winter—and were decayed by Spring. And in the Spring it rained, and the huge sloppy flower I had painted on the glass—with my son—washed off. I felt demoralized, sometimes, looking out at the trashy garden I had made. And far from home. The more time passed, the less and less was Ban. Something that could be written down.

10. Prepare yourselves. I collaborated with Claudia Rankine on Stories of Brown Girlhood—but dropped the ball. It was too hard to keep writing the stories and also it was the same story, again and again. It was the story of a girl on the floor of the world; perhaps for Claudia it was a similar thing. She had a beautiful handbag and a family; I felt that I had ruined everything and watched as even my handbag fell apart. I do not mean that I ruined the collaboration but rather that I did not have the kind of life that supported the work with charcoal and narrative forms. When the opportunity came to present my work at a literary event, I was mortified at the thought of reading Ban. I went to the thrift store and bought some red fabric that felt and moved like silk. My mother sewed me a loose bag with a drawstring at the throat. Two weeks later, I removed my clothes. I climbed into the throat. Inside the bag, the lights of the studio were very soft. Another writer dragged me onto the stage. In the meat sack, I made a gesture-posture set for Ban. I pulled the drawstring tight and convulsed—spasmed—for Ban. Later that night, I wrote a sensorimotor sequence for Ban. I made a theory of narrative and the nervous system for Ban. I made a cadence for Ban. I made a syntax for Ban. The error of the performance was not that I did these things—but rather—that the discharge of something long held—in the body—does not—affect—or modulate—the resurgence—of a latent—and vehement (British) Far Right. My mistake is that I

perform works intended for a European audience—in California—and that I do not have the courage or means to go home.

11. In December 2012, a girl returning from the cinema in New Delhi, having watched the *Life of Pi*, was caught and raped—gutted with a steel pipe—on a bus—then thrown to the ground. Near the Vasunt Kunj enclave—with its Dubai skyline rising up behind the flaps and hemp rooves of the market—and about 10 minutes from the Indira Gandhi airport—the girl lay dying on the ground. She lay on the ground for 40 minutes—twitching—making low sounds—then none at all—diminishing—before anyone called the police. I thought about those 40 minutes and compared them to the fictive—12 hours—that Ban lay on the ground. What was in the work—as an image—had appeared beyond it—as a scene. I thought about the crowd that gathered to watch as—the girl—the Fearless One—as they called her, aftewards—began to die; a black rope and other materials extended from her body towards them—according to witness accounts. Does the body of the witness discharge something too? At that moment, I stopped writing Ban.

12. And there I lay down on the ground.

13. And this was the part of the project that could not be completed in the same place that the project was held. And this was what happened when the project fell away and all I was left with were the materials themselves and what the materials wanted was to be crushed and to be returned to the earth and ultimately to be set on fire—to receive the pink lightning—in every part of themselves—but I knew that if I did this, if I continued to write—like this—then I myself—would not be able—to return.

Pratt Institute, New York, 2013.

Auto-sacrifice (Notes) --

1. *Pink Lightning for Ban*

"The day of the riot dawns bright and lazy with a giant silky cloud sloughing off above the rooves."

"The mouth of the riot is a stretch of road."

Pink lightning fills the borough like a graph. All day, I graph the bandages, race passion and chunks of dirt to Ban—plant-like, she's stretching then contracting on the ground.

Three streets over, a mixed group nears a house. Their faces are pressed to the blood-flecked window, banging their forehead on the glass. Inside the house, a woman arranges the meat on a tarp. She tucks and pins the shroud behind its ears with quick-moving hands, looking up from time to time at the crowd that's gathered to spit on the window and call.

That night, I dreamed of exiting the subway at the interface a car would make with the M25. The commuters were processing around a semi-rural roundabout, their hands on imaginary steering wheels, their wing-backed loafers shuffling on the tarmac, the black road, like wheels. Evening Standards tucked sharply beneath their arms.

The dream requires something of me.

It requires me to acknowledge that my creature (Ban) is over-written by a psychic history that is lucid, astringent, witty. No longer purely mine.

2. *Meat forest: 1979*

Ban fulfills the first criterium of monstrosity simply by degrading: by emitting bars of light from her teeth and nails, when the rain sweeps over her then back again.

I like how the rain is indigo, like a tint that reveals the disease process in its inception.

Above her, the pink lightning is branched—forked—in five places.

A brown ankle sparkles on the ground.

Genital life gives way to bubbles, the notebook of a body's two eyes.

Like a person in an ancient pose, I lean in a L-shaped posture over the counter: flat back, rump displayed to any passer-by, blood dripping down the backs of my thighs. They don't see me. I clean the street until all that's left is a ring of oily foam, the formal barrier of a bad snow. Are you sick and tired of running away?

Then lie down.

Invert yourself above a ditch or stream beneath a bright blue sky.

Then pull yourself up from your knees to clean.

Clean the street until all that's left is a ring of oily foam, the formal barrier of a bad snow.

It snows that April for a few minutes, early in the day. Children walking on the Southall Broadway open their mouths to receive the aluminium snowflakes. In their bright pink and chocolate brown dresses, tucked beneath the heavy blue coats, these immigrant children are dazzled by the snow, even though they were born here, a train-ride from a city tilted to receive the light, its sprig bending over in the window of the pretty bank.

Many years later, I return. To place a daffodil on the Uxbridge Road.

Is zinc an element? It's a sheen. Spread it on the ankle of Ban.

Is there a copper wire? Is there a groin? Make a mask for Ban.

3. *What* is *Ban?*

Ban is a mixture of dog shit and bitumen (ash) scraped off the soles of running shoes: Puma, Reebok, Adidas.

Looping the city, Ban is a warp of smoke.

To summarize, she is the parts of something re-mixed as air: integral, rigid air, circa 1972–1979. She's a girl. A black girl in an era when, in solidarity, Caribbean and Asian Brits self-defined as black. A black (brown) girl encountered in the earliest hour of a race riot, or what will become one by nightfall.

April 23rd, 1979: by morning, anti-Nazi campaigner, Blair Peach, will be dead.

It is, in this sense, a real day: though Ban is unreal. She's both dead and never living: the part, that is, of life that is never given: an existence. What, for example, is born in England, but is never, not even on a cloudy day, English?

Under what conditions is a birth not recognized as a birth?

Answer: *Ban.*

And from Ban: "banlieues."

(The former hunting grounds of King Henry VIII. Earth-mounds. Oaks split into several parts by a late-century lightning storm.) These suburbs are, in places, leafy and industrial; the Nestle factory spools a milky, lilac effluent into the Grand Union canal that runs between

Hayes and Southall. Ban is nine. Ban is seven. Ban is ten. Ban is a girl walking home from school just as a protest starts to escalate. Pausing at the corner of the Uxbridge Road, she hears something: the far-off sound of breaking glass. Is it coming from her home or is it coming from the street's distant clamor? Faced with these two sources of a sound she instinctively links to violence, the potential of violent acts, Ban lies down. She folds to the ground. This is syntax.

Psychotic, fecal, neural, wild: the auto-sacrifice begins, endures the night: never stops: goes on.

As even more time passes, as the image or instinct to form this image desiccates, I prop a mirror, then another, on the ground for Ban.

A cyclical and artificial light falls upon her in turn: pink, gold, amber then pink again. Do the mirrors deflect evil? Perhaps they protect her from a horde of boys with shaved heads or perhaps they illuminate—in strings of weak light—the part of the scene when these boys, finally, arrive.

The left hand covered in a light blue ash. The ash is analgesic, data, soot, though when it rains, Ban becomes leucine, a bulk, a network of dirty lines that channel starlight, presence, boots. Someone walks towards her, for example, then around her, then away.

I want to lie down in the place I am from: on the street I am from.

In the rain. Next to the ivy. As I did, on the border of Pakistan and India: the two Punjabs. Nobody sees someone do this. I want to feel it in my body—the root cause.

4. *Cobra Notes for Ban*

I want a literature that is not made from literature. A girl walks home in the first minutes of a race riot, before it might even be called that— the sound of breaking glass as equidistant, as happening/coming from the street and from her home.

What loops the ivy-asphalt/glass-girl combinations? Abraded as it goes? I think, too, of the curved, passing sound that has no fixed source. In a literature, what would happen to the girl? I write, instead, the increment of her failure to orient, to take another step. And understand. She is collapsing to her knees then to her side in a sovereign position.

Notes for Ban, 2012: a year of sacrifice and rupture, murderous roses blossoming in the gardens of immigrant families with money problems, citizens with a stash: and so on. Eat a petal and die. Die if you have to. See: end-date, serpent-gate. Hole. I myself swivel around and crouch at the slightest unexpected sound.

When she turned her face to the ivy, I saw a cube of foil propped between the vines. Posture made a circuit from the ivy to her face. The London street a tiny jungle: dark blue, slick and shimmering a bit, from the gold/brown tights she was wearing beneath her skirt. A girl stops walking and lies down on a street in the opening scene of a riot. Why? At points it rains. In a novel that no one writes or thinks of writing, the rain falls in lines and dots upon her. In the loose genetics of what makes this street real, the freezing cold, vibrating weather sweeping through south-east England at 4 p.m. on an April afternoon is very painful. Sometimes there is a day and sometimes there is a day reduced to its symbolic elements: a cup of broken glass; the Queen's portrait on a thin bronze coin; dosage; rain.

This is why a raindrop indents the concrete with atomic intensity. This is why the dark green, glossy leaves of the ivy are so green: multiple kinds of green: as night falls on the "skirt." The outskirts of London: *les banlieues.*

5. *I wanted to re-imagine the boundary*

Perhaps I should say that I grew up partly in Ruislip. The Park Woods that bounded it were rimmed, themselves, with land forms that kept in the boar. I used to go directly to those masses and lie down on them, subtly above a city but beneath the plate of leaves, in another world.

One morning I went there though it was raining.

To soften this scene would require time travel, which I am not prepared to do. I am not prepared to take off my clothes. I am not prepared to charter or re-organize the cosmic symbols of Sikhism, Anglican Christianity and the Hindu faith. One night, I went home, and my hands were caked in dirt and dew. My skirt was up around my ears. My legs were cold. The insides of my eyes were cold. The bath I took, I couldn't get it hot enough. That night, my eyes turned blue.

More recently, I've been obsessed with the image of a dark-skinned girl walking home from school.

Imagine your fingertips are animals that still carry the imprint of a plant memory.

And the veins of the nearby plants flood with sugar. The sugar and the sky suck the body of a black woman. They surge towards her through the mud and air. Pinned there, scrawled, like a name. A woman (girl) so black she radiates a limited consciousness. In this scene without depth, she is supine, lifting her arms very carefully then setting them down; an image that is never exhausted, though I write it again and again. With a careful hand.

How the street tilts and the rain and blood slide into the gutter below the pavement's lip. A dress slides off and is received by the white space beneath the ivy. Is the street a letterbox? Is the night your mouth? A long black hair is carried to Yeading High Street on the sole of a shoe. And it's there behind *The White Stag*, a skinhead pub on the border with Hayes, that the hair sheds off. At this moment, like a delicate clock, the difficult music of another century, the riot begins—a distant roar, a van with orange stripes—a strobe.

I made the ivy go faster like a carpet or rug I could pull.

Ban turns her head to the wall.

Imagine a cloud of milk as it dissipates, spilled on a London street in an act of protest.

Imagine mica glinting in the oily curd of the pavement.

Imagine that the rough, pink tip of a girl's tongue slips out, extending to the ivy's salt—for nourishment.

What did Ban do that outweighed art? What kind of art did she produce?

Returning to the U.S., I lay down in the mud, removing my clothes and exposing my body with its waist and hips and suitcase of limbs.

Above me, in a bush of late summer flowers—white pom-poms with deep green leaves—migrating finches made a choral sound.

From one angle, Ban is slick, like the emerald or indigo tint of ring feathers. From another she is a kerosene patch set on fire with a careless match.

The sun burns and heals.

But it's time to go home. As we coast up the estuary, veering left and north towards Heathrow, I can see the Southall water tower and the golden, balloon-shaped minaret of the Sikh temple. I look down as we fly over and there, close enough to touch, is the set of *Ban*. I describe the creamy clouds in my notebook, how they emit dark silver beams of light.

I analyze my glimpse of the asphalt.

Nevertheless, when it was time for such a thing, I could not bear to be touched—by another person.

Ban opens her mouth for the spores that pour from the early morning sun on April 23rd, a Monday morning in 1979—just as the rioters are eating their breakfast, an egg on a piece of toast, with not a thought— of riot—in their heart.

6. *Notes Toward a Race Riot Scene*

In April 1979, I was ten years old.

This is a short talk about vectors. It's about Brueghel's Icarus. It's about a girl walking home from school at the exact moment her neighbor laces up his Doc Martens, tight. It's about a partial and irrelevant nudity. It's about the novel as a form that processes the part of a scene that doesn't function as an image, but as the depleted, yet still livid mixture of materials that a race riot is made from. Think of the sky. Think of the clear April day with its cardigans and late afternoon rain shower. Think of the indigo sky lowering over London like a lid. Think of Blair Peach, the anti-racism campaigner and recent emigrant from New Zealand, who will die before this day is out.

Think about a cyborg to get to the immigrant.

Think of a colony. Think of the red and white daikon radishes in a tilted box on the pavement outside Dokal and Sons, on the corner of the Uxbridge Road and Lansbury Drive. Think of the road, which here we call asphalt: there, it is bitty. It is a dark silver with milky oil seams. A patch up job, *Labour* still in power, but not for long. It's 1979, St. George's Day, and the Far Right has decided to have its annual meeting in a council-run meeting hall in Southall, Middlesex, a London suburb in which it would be rare—nauseating—to see a white face.

To see anyone, actually. Everyone's indoors. Everyone can tell what's coming. It's not a riot, at this point, but a simple protest in an outlying area of London, an immigrant suburb: a *banlieue*. Everyone knows to board the glass up, draw the curtains and lie down. Lie down between the hand-sewn quilts shipped from India in a crate then covered in an outer cotton case stitched to the padding with a fine pink thread. The quilts smell of an antiseptic powder, an anti-fungal, Mars. We lie down beneath the blankets in front of the fire. It's 1979, so there's a small gas fire and a waist-high fridge, where we keep our milk and our bread and our cheese, right there, in the living room. It's 1979, and so I live in Hayes, though in two months, we'll put our house on the market and move.

Move away. As would you.

7. *Ban en Banlieues (suburban)*

A puff of diesel fumes on an orbital road.

The country outside London, with its old parks and labyrinths of rhododendron or azalea.

Futile and tropical pinks in a near-constant downpour of green, black and silver rain.

In the forest surrounding London, a light ice falls through the trees.

Like glitter.

A snake, aspen-colored, bright yellow with green stripes, slips through the bracken, its pink eyes open and black diamond-shaped irises blinking on then off. In frozen time, ancient beings emerge with the force of reptiles. In the forest, time and weather are so mixed up, a trope of bedtime stories, bottom-up processing, need. I need the snake to stop the news. This is the news: a girl's body is dressed and set: still yet trembling, upon a rise in the forest. There are stars. Now it's night. Time is coming on hard. The snake slips over her leg, her brown ankle. She's wearing shoes, maroon patent leather shoes with a low heel and three slim buckles, but no socks.

Whoever dressed her was in a hurry.

Imagine the scene: a forest outside of London, 10 p.m.

An April snowfall, the ground still coppery, gold. A snake has escaped from time: a water box, a shelf. Volatile, starving, it senses a parallel self, the girl's body emitting a solar heat, absorbed in the course of a lifetime but now discharging, pushing off. Without thought, below thought, it moves towards her through the rusted trees.

8. *Inversions for Ban*

"To ban someone is to say that no-one may harm him." —Agamben.

A "monstrous hybrid of human and animal, divided between the forest and the city." (*Ban*.) To be: "banned from the city" and thus: *en banlieues*: a part of the perimeter. In this sense, to study the place where the city dissolves is to study the wolf. Is this why some of my best friends have come from the peninsula of Long Island?

To ban, to sentence.

To abandon is thus to write prose. "Already dead." Nude. A "wulfesheud" upon a form. The form is the body—in the most generic way I could possibly use that word. The nude body spills color. Blue nude, green nude. The nudes of pre-history in a pool of chalk in an Ajanta cave. Agamben's thought familiar to me, already, from the exchange of Arjun and Krishan on the battlefield. I should stop writing now.

What do the wolf and the schizophrenic have in common?

Here, extreme snow. I mean fire. The extreme snow makes me neutral about this first intact fragment. Of Ban. A novel of the race riot, "Ban." Nude studies/charcoal marks: wired to the mouth of a pig. A boar. Some of the work is set in the outlying, wooded regions of Greater London, where King Henry VIII had his hunting grounds. As a girl, I would lie down in my coat and trousers in the snow upon an embankment of earth: engineered, centuries before, to keep the meat in.

41

I wanted to write a book that was like lying down.

That took some time to write, that kept forgetting something, that took a diversion: from which it never returned.

I wanted to write a book on a butcher's table in New Delhi: the shop-front open to the street, a bare light bulb swinging above the table and next to it a hook.

Swinging from that hook in the window, I wanted to write a book. Inverted, corrupted, exposed to view: a person writes a book in their free time, calling that time what they want to call it.

I wanted to write a book about England.

I wanted to write a book about lying on the floor of England. I wanted to return to England. I went to England. I was born in England. I lived in a house in England until I was thirty years old. My parents were English. I was English. After 1984, we all shared the same nationality, but by 2006 or 7, this was no longer true. Between September 2010 and late December 2012, I studied a piece of the earth, no longer or wider than a girl's body prone upon it. The asphalt. As dusk fell: violet/amber—and filled—with the reflected lights coming from the discs, the tiny mirrors, positioned in the ivy as she "slept."

On a balcony or street.

The asphalt's green stars, the shed parts of a ragged elm come Spring.

Ban is a portal, a vortex, a curl: a mixture of clockwise and anti-clockwise movements in the sky above the street. I study the vapor as it rises, accumulates then starts to move. How a brisk wind organizes the soot or casings and bits of bark into whorls.

9. *Notes for a novel never written*

Ban dreams of being eaten alive by wolves.

Ban has tickets from the West End, and playbills, that will surely be worth something some day.

Are those two words? Someday. Tucked into a suitcase. Or sent in a crate. This pure banality, the sending of household supplies by freight, is an emigrant act. A form of nudity. And not a novel-length account.

Notes.

With some anger, the kind that builds up over years, in the absence of social services, I write sentences for days. Day three, day four, day nine. Days you never see, chucking back your Bombay Sapphire gin on the patio. Define patio. You could be naked out back and no one would see. Nobody. Where the two vowels ooze geneticity. Or display it. Just as the body without clothes on is analagous to a race mark. I asked my nine-year-old son why he wore his T-shirt to the outdoor pool. He said: "Mom, I think there might be some racists here." I wanted to tell him: "Honey. Honey...."

Ban is lying in the dirt, all sticky from her ice.

Ban is alone in a café as an adult, dispersing the gazes of others with nothing more than a pen and cup of coffee.

She's in India. Always India, where café culture varies, region by region, to be: almost non-existent. In the part she is from. Where she is. In a Sector 17 café. Writing in a place where everyone else is eating a quick breakfast. Like a tourist or office worker. Or the boss, taking his time and even smoking, smoking a rolled-up cigarette as he drinks his chai, staring hard at Ban when she stops writing. "Yes, ma'am. Cold coffee?" Ban licks the foam off her spoon then bends her head to the page again.

But what is she writing? In my own way, from this wet perch, one foot chained to the cage, I am staring too. A parrot. A shabby, vivid bird, pecking at her words. In times of great freedom, when the writing comes, I fly back to my own writing with what she knows. This is another reason not to write novels. Or read.

To summarize, I don't want to have sex ever again in my life.

I don't want it if it means partnering with a white man. A man who takes your polka-dotted dress from you and puts it on. Or leaves it on the brown plastic tray with the remnants of breakfast, outside the door, for a late morning clean-up. Why, in fact, would anyone disrobe with such casual proficiency, then lie down like that, with their legs and arms in the air? Like a baby? Why would a person get naked for a person with whom you do not share culture? (Ban).

But if Ban is a fundamentalist, if Ban converts, at some point, to the radical ideal of the body as somehow untouchable, the very thing you cannot reach, then at some point, she'll have to take off her kit.

Sometimes I see Ban in the dirt of the place she is from.

Ban lying down on a sidewalk in London.

Without resistance. Beneath the ivy. At night.

Like bones before they are bones. Like eyes in the time that follows talking.

10. *Chrysalis Notes, India*

And there I lay down.

And filled it. With gold, red and orange "blooms." And dirt. Nobody saw.

The most realistic rendering I could make of this experience—an experience that unfolded in the heat—would be to crawl on my knees around a cone of dirt, the reddish, pale yellow dirt of that place. The cone would be displaced, ready-made, a tip in the street—as if a hole had been dug nearby.

"I walk through the summer forest. It's abandoned. Only five or six flowers are securely in bloom. A white one, a yellow one, a red one, and three light blue/purple ones. In late July, I was walking on a gemstone path carved into the side of the mountain. "Mica." "Quartz." Nouns are magical to an immigrant, fundamental to a middle class education."

I made a mark in the dirt where something was.

A blinking cursor made of minerals and concrete and the evening rain.

I ate whatever was on my plate, in a basement café on the campus of Temple University, on the other side of the continent. The notes I made were like wings, the wet parts that broke off. To leak a seam.

Next to the ivy was a sheet of paper, throbbing where it froze. The frost on each green leaf. A dark or glossy leaf with creamy and rigid veins.

A philosophy of the street in which nothing happens, outwardly.

The roar of the race riot dims. Ban is crumpled like a tulip: there. A wetness, that is, with limbs. There are subtle movements: ventral and dorsal (muscular) twitches. This is the sensorimotor sequence. This is voltage: the body routed through its sounds: groans, murmurs, shouts. A brown girl on the floor of the world: mirrored or banked by flares of electricity in an incipient, late April storm. In the lapse between frames, the ivy-asphalt is weirdly green, illuminated by lightning bolts. Do these bright colors have their own autonomy or generative power? I don't know.

Where's the group? I hate the group.

Genital life gives way to bubbles, the notebook of a body's two eyes. Are you sick and tired of running away? I pull myself up from my knees to clean.

I clean the street until all that's left is a ring of oily foam, the formal barrier of a bad snow.

This is the snow: I think often about low-levels of racism, the very parts of a social system or institution that are hard to address, precisely because they are non-verbal—a greater trigger for schizophrenia in immigrant populations: in women, that is, than larger events, the race riot, for example, with its capacity: to be analyzed.

Many years later, I return.

I place a daffodil on the Uxbridge Road. It's early April, not quite the anniversary of Ban.

11. *Nude page for Ban*

I attach: a nude page for Ban.

I did not know how to scan in the page and send it to you. You had said I could send you something in a note form. The page, as you will see, is empty. The page at home is the same, but smudged. "Ban" is a puff of diesel. Something like a smudge, already dispersing. A warp of smoke looping around the orbital road surrounding London. So, the page I have in front of me is this page but with some soot, taken from the car exhaust pipe and smeared on the page.

Could I ask you, or someone else you know, who does not mind getting dirty, to take some charcoal or soot and, casually, smudge the page—and this be my page to submit?

Because nude pages are smudged. Prehensile. Dirty. A way to predict writing but not writing itself.

12. *Sun and moon for Ban*

When I was about to emigrate from England, my uncle Roshan, an astrologer and palmist who had lived for some time in the President's palace in New Delhi, and later the Prime Minister's, told me not to go.

In front of a small group of advisors, he told Indira Gandhi that she would be killed by two men standing next to her at a certain point in the moon's arc across the sky. Evicted from the residence, he became, briefly, famous, when his prediction came true. Similarly, in a thick Indian accent, on the plush green sofa with its repeating leaf pattern, he said: "There is a giant snake eating its tail above America." We looked at a map in the Children's Encyclopedia that my father had bought from a travelling salesman in 1977. Uncle Roshan pointed to Toronto and drew a line, with his near-black fingertip, to Manhattan—the zone to avoid. I flew to Rochester, a small city on the shore of Lake Ontario. The day before I left, he made a holy fire in our living room and bathed me in the fragrant smoke, chanting a mantra to protect me.

From the violence to come.

The sun and the moon produce an intense light in the sky. On the aeroplane to America, I write a short story about Harrede, a French girl who scrapes a plate of spaghetti onto her lap when an older male diner and his wife stare at her uncombed hair in a restaurant. It is a true story, told to me before I leave—by Andy McMahon, a tall boy in a red leather jacket who wants to make friends. But I can't make friends. I can't have sex with a boy.

Instead, I emigrate.

To speak from my organs in a fiction without end. "Organ-speech," as Rose writes. Wrote: a sound or act that "serves to halt, even as it exposes, the ceaseless dispersal of the text."

That serves to halt.

Even as it exposes.

The ceaseless dispersal.

Of the text.

13. *Five fictions for Ban*

[1] "We walk through the rusted bracken to the lido, to the place where the Park Woods give way to a cultivated beach.

The darkness beneath the trees is a treatment, something a person might seek out to modify other sensations. It's a thick balm made from summer herbs and cooked in a pan. Comfrey turns the skin green where it sits. And if London, in turn, is packed inside the remnants of this forest, I can describe it only because I lived there and recall these themes, which are not themes. Returning, I change at Baker Street and take the Metropolitan line north. Where it ends I get off. Start walking."

—Ban, who lived for the first nine years of her life at 76 Lansbury Drive, Hayes, Middlesex (U.K.) and so cuts back one, revving, slipping on the wet grass, to begin. Will you give a hand to Ban? Do you have a sentiment, do you class? Let me tell you before you extend yourself that Ban is disgusting. Let me tell you that Ban is a difficult person to love, full of transience. I could tell you things about Ban.

[2] "Back at the house, there were some sugar crystals on the carpet.

I knew I should hoover them up before they got ground in. My husband slamming doors, banging around, you should do this, you should do that. My son threw in some white bin-liners. I was like— thanks? But later, when it was time to make something to eat, I'd lost track. I didn't know whether to defrost the meat."

—Ban's friend at KFC, during lunch on a plaza bench. Ban is pure sympathy, still in uniform, one of the girls. That's something that's come clear to me over the years that I've known of her, through others and finally, though it was too late, in person: Ban. Who wants: to carve out her body from her body, to conceive herself with a human life in mind. Whatever. I can't bring myself to do much more than tell how she lived. Then died. Ban on a bench, passing, nodding, brushing the crumbs from the burger off her rough red skirt.

[3] "We wanted to look for bottles, the tiny bottles we had heard were left in the roots of oak trees by elves.

My dad said: "Be back by four." And Thippy and I leaped out of the car into the rain. It was raining, but only lightly and we had anoraks on. I'd recalled the haystacks I'd once seen, at the very end of the park, where a gate was and a white home with a thousand sparkling windows. Once, in the private meadow edging the park, I'd seen riders in their scarlet coats. Their horses had coats. I'd shouted: "Oi! Over here! Yoo hoo!" longing to touch the dark brown fur and feel the warm breath on my face. Thus, in the azalea maze next to the car park, digging with sticks beneath the hedge, I said: *come on.* Thippy was a Sikh boy with hair down to his waist. Out of view, he took off his pint-sized turban and let it fall. We pretended we were sisters, as we sometimes did at Balfours, buying six ounce bags of lemon sherbert with pennies stolen from the kitchen jar. It took two hours, that afternoon, to reach the haystacks and during our walk, we understood, in our hearts, that returning to the car would be just as bad as going back later. When we reached the gate, it was pouring and our hands were blue on the backs of them from the cold. A creamy mist had risen from the grass. From this mist appeared a horse, a completely white horse with muddy legs, and the rider tugged it so it came to where we screamed: "Horsey! Over here, horsey!" And let us pet it, forever, chatting, a man. When we got back to the car, we were wet. We got into the car, a blue Ford Cortina dented silver from my father's many accidents. We got into the car and in slow motion my father twisted from the chest up, from the driver's seat, to hit my face so hard the side of my head hit the window.

At this moment, I became Ban. When Thippy grew up, and his own father dragged him home from the school disco at Villier's High School, and beat him on his legs and back, he became a Sikh fundamentalist. What choice did he have? He'd grown a beard by seventeen, and refused to meet my eyes on the rare occasions his parents forced him to come to our house for a Friday night dinner. He wore a black turban with a saffron headband and when he grew up, he bought the house next to his parents and they built a corridor between the two. But what I've left out is his brother, a boy I knew in childhood who also made me Ban. Not because he accompanied me; on the contrary, because he, too, made me weep. He wasn't a boy. When we were eight, he was eighteen. When we were ten, he was twenty."

—A story of Ban's childhood. Has Ban described the countryside well, as it extends from the immigrant township built on the slope beneath the Nestle factory, but above the canal, where children swam in summer? Has Ban described the pink flowers against the dark silver background of the labyrinth, fragrant with juniper and other rotting things? Answer: No. Ban fails portraiture. Ban fails life, which is color. It is "costume *and* valence." It is something more than this.

[4] "It's getting dusky over the Makhatini flats.

Last night, I told P. I did not want to continue seeing him when I returned to New York. I believe, in breaking up with him, I compared myself to a Safeway rotisserie chicken. I said I didn't want to be one. Then I put down the phone and went back to drinking my rooibos tea. Yes and no. I should have asked her to make some coffee instead."

—In the mid 90s, Ban went to the Zulu Homeland, to visit a childhood friend from Hayes, a suburban girl of mixed race (half Trinidadian-Indian, half white) who married an Afrikaaner she met in Capetown. I can't name that girl, or say why she left the suburbs, as Ban, in her phone call to another friend, the person I ultimately interviewed, didn't go into details. In the notes I took, Ban comes across as a person with a soft heart, but what I slice off is the "she." Who, in this day and age, refers to a person for the first time as "her"? Who is this "her"? Is Ban a "black" person, using a mode of address she would not dare to in the United Kingdom? Is Ban black? Though now she is black. And flecked with silver. At the bottom of a river. On the street. "I have excellent clothes," Ban once wrote to her friend, a letter I kept when it was given to me, not wanting to be rude.

[5] "Mother of my soul."

—Towards the end of her life, in her early forties, still very beautiful despite her age, dark brown hair knotted with paintbrushes in a tatty bun above C7, the last bone of the spine as it goes down through the neck, Ban returned to India, where her ancestors were from, and lay down, as close as she could get, next to the border with Pakistan. A few feet away, under the gaze of a military presence, two guards a few feet away from the Wagah checkpoint, she simply did this (lie down), then stood up and with a long stick torn from a nearby tree, though the area is desolate, marked the outline that was left. Then she re-filled this shape with marigolds purchased, earlier that day, from the Shiva temple of a village further in. It must have been a Monday. Then she sat down next to this body and placed a hand on the place where its chest would be, and another upon on her own. I began to write on Ban. It was this writing that led me further in, to the place I did not want to be, Ban's soul. "Mother of my soul," she wrote in an early notebook, what in England is still called a Diary, "You're so very bright." What did Ban mean? My question was innocent. I was innocent. But Ban, in a sense, was waiting for me, in the darkness of the border, no longer proximal but centered, arms waving in a blur, waiting with everything that was wrong.

14. *Paranoia and the body*

"People are looking at you." "Animals are looking at you."

I'm reading Adorno in the middle of the night on April 23rd, 2013: Ban's night, as it is, I realized, somewhere between all the Shakespeare references; the anniversary of the riot I am writing upon. About. 10:33 p.m. Ban is almost there now—a sheer frost on her skirt and eyebrows. "Your eyebrows are so ugly. Did anyone ever tell you that?"

I want to think about the body becoming a kind of food for the street. Irreducible.

"I put out your light." "I put you in the garbage."

It's weird to gather these statements. For years now, I've been thinking about schizophrenia and disgust. How the capacity of a schizophrenic to recognize disgust in another person's face, the person looking at them, is actually the thing that's workable. You can train the schizophrenic to recognize other facial expressions based on their ability to respond to that one. Anhedonia, for example, the negative symptom of schizophrenia, is "the abyss between sentences," as Gail Scott writes. Decontextualized.

I wrote about this subject for many years.

I had no sense of being seen or observed by anyone as I wrote. Perhaps this was a problem too.

My family lived in an end terrace with a coal chute in the garden and a rusted out, abandoned Morris Minor with a shattered windscreen propped against the back fence. Next door lived Stephen Whitby, a member of the National Front's youth league. With regularity, he'd empty out the milk bottles of our Gujrati and Kenyan neighbors, filling them with an unrelenting supply of urine before putting them back on the step. He must have woken before dawn to do this. Red top for cream, silver for lowfat. Is he on Facebook?

Once, a man was beating his wife. Stephen Whitby climbed over the wall and banged his head on the window. He spat at the window then thumped it with his hand, screaming: "You fucking Paki!" He screamed: "Go back home, you bleeding animal!" The man stopped beating his wife, then resumed.

Adorno substituted people for animals; I feel cautious and sad reading his words in the middle of the night, studying the body for Ban.

Why?

To "reduce the living body." [E. Grosz].

To reach the point at which: "life rubs up against matter, its inner core." And thus to analyze nudity, in a text, as friction, the sacrifice gone wrong: but also: the normalizing contact with membranes of all kinds—plant, brush, nettles, ivy, asphalt, skin. What is the function of a non-genital nudity in a work of narrative? How can the body perform something in a new way—something that belongs neither to the scene nor to history? Note from the labyrinth: 2.b.

On the second day, pre-sky. Thinking, also, of bodies without shelter. How I woke up in India and looked down; we'd arrived at night. I looked down from the window of a third floor flat to see body outlines, stirring, uncovering, shifting—beneath the soft/hard cardboard and aluminum layers.

In this way, I want swarming movements mixed with static forms.

Like Henry Moore's sculptures in the Denver Botanical Gardens.

Research: Upper European, dark green plants. And molten bronze.

Focus hard on life to write a novel.

Try not to be afraid.

Perhaps for one night.

You don't have to be afraid.

15. *Notes for Ban: an infantile bank*

Or diptych.

A presentation, pre-soaked. Quiet. It's so quiet before a book begins.

So quiet that when my nervous system hurts, so does the sentence, because that's all we have: each other. The sentence and I. We cope.

Met Andrew W. at Coda and after we'd settled down with our millet scones and tea, we made a pact to meet in Colorado, or virtually, a year from now, with novels.

Novels set in the U.K. and that we have not written yet. Why? Some ideas: "Lazy." "Time." Andrew makes a list and when we part, I tuck it in my bag, which rips where the arm of it, the strap, meets the red cloth of the torso. Who wants to pay through the nose for new accommodations? Not I.

This is a bank for sentences.

All the tellers are out to lunch. Customers purge on Newsweek and cappuccinno in a central lobby designed so poorly that sometimes, before the agent returns, they leave. Some places, like the sloping bar-stool seats McDonalds pioneered in the late 1980s, eject you from your childhood position.

Anything but talk about Ban.

I would talk about pedophilia before I talked about Ban. Her left leg or arm. As a child, I lay down on the bed like a sentence not written yet. Out came a pen. Out came paper. I have a memory of the paper slipping under my hips, for example.

A memory of public events that supersedes, perhaps, the grid of touch.

Flowers, electricity, and even herbs. I place them in a vase. I flip the switch. A foreign body is a frequency. It's a body flaring with violet light when you look away from the sheet and its matching pillow. These are notes, so I don't have to go there. I don't have to lie down with you. And I don't.

Just as I never write.

Just as I prevent myself from writing at all costs.

Just as I do not love.

Just as I substitute fiction for prose, and prose for the sentences that, like animals.

Like schizophrenics.

Like wolves.

Emit light. Perceptible to the ones who also. Lie down on the ground. Lie down on the ground like that.

16. *Love Note for Ban*

I think of a person I loved between the years 2004 and 2007, which were not years.

They were hours. "Little hours," as Andrew called them in Coda, a word that bears repeating. I think of how I lay down on the ground for him, thinking he would come, with coffee, and a blanket, but how, when morning came, I had frozen into a new position.

On a bank, where the stems transplant themselves upon our skin.

Because we're dead. We lay down on the riverbank and never got up again. Our ******* turned into red flowers that flared then rotted away, in the banal image of the body's reproductive system appearing outside it, as a gent. The yellow stamen that stabilized the parts of the page that looked boring, when we glanced down at the page, just lying there, with its legs open.

A book of time, for time and because of it.

A book for recovery from an illness. A book that repeats a sentence until that sentence recuperates its power to attract, or touch, other sentences.

A book as much poetry as it is a forbidden or unfunded area of research. The first thing to go when the bank fails. When the bank manager books his vacation to Costa Rica and blanks it out. His commitment. The strength of the British pound. An attendant menagerie of quotients, HR tips, and downtown rent.

I think of Roualt, who burned his paintings "due to criticism."

I think of Barbara, who went to the Art Institute of Chicago sixty years ago. She's eighty, I think. Her husband has dementia. He's an alcoholic, in fact, and we're meeting about that. We're meeting in a room. Barbara and I annoy the group when we veer off into conversations about art. Barbara says: "I painted rocks at the Art Institute." She says: "Sometimes I can't draw but I get some nice lines." I invite her to my house and somehow she drives from Fort Collins, shaking like a leaf on its stem. It's Barbara who tells me about Roualt, and about her marriage, which dominated this other part of life. Its feathers. Feral moments so valuable you never share them with anyone else.

Like finances.

Like the writings of Melanie Klein. They are a deep orange with a cream border and though I don't open the book, I keep it next to me as I write.

I go to the café to write, but am boxed in by two women close to my age.

A bit younger or older. I can't tell. The first one says: "He makes me feel like I'm smart and uber-attractive. Sure, I'm thirty-seven but I look like I'm thirty, don't I? I have to show my ID every time I buy alcohol." And then: "Here's what you'll see. About twenty per cent of the females will be uber-pregnant. The thighs, lard ass." In time, I understand that they are discussing an up-coming high school reunion. "They'll be pregnant," says the second woman, "and fat.

Unattractively fat."

Perhaps, I think, I'll set the bulk of my book in Haberdasher's Aske's School for Girls.

Perhaps Ban will be dark, but also crystalline, like a high-school vampire. Like blending something in a pan.

The paper that lines the pan.

For cookies.

"I hate cookies almost as much as I hate white people."

Says Ban, to begin.

To write a sentence with content more volatile that what contains it.

So that the page is shiny, wet and hard.

So that sentences are indents not records; the soulful presence of a vibrant man or girl rather than persistence.

Their capacity to touch you in the present time.

17. *Anamorphia for Ban*

I wrote these notes not to be included in a book but because of it, right now.

If it's love that links you to the earth, then I am writing these dull notes on a cloud. Give me another sip of that baby. Give me another slug of that leg. Writing these sentences in the sky, I'm wearing my very best sky-diving outfit: a negligee from Loughborough. I bought it on Ashby Street about a million years ago. Far above England, Wales, and then the sea, as we head towards Newfoundland on a sub-volcano swerve: I think about schizophrenia and make the race connection. Cos it's easy, and at this point well known. But you might not know it. And I didn't know it at the time.

My confidence faltered though these, below, I retained, for Ban:

A pseudonym, a stupid fragment. Mint tea. I don't write for you, you write for me.

That is a schizophrenic sentence.

I hate white people.

That is another sentence.

I hate white people in groups.

That is definitely borderline schizophrenic, but as the person was born in Hayes, on the west part of town, in the complex of terraced houses behind the botanical garden, it's understandable. The person was born in Hayes eight years before the race riot of 1979, which was subdued. A violence like snowflakes from under the bed, three maroon silk-covered duvets padding the space from the legs to the floor, though it never snows in England. Though it does now.

A fragment with its sticky edges rotating in a wet, dark space.

That's a snowflake if you ask me. You asking me? Then use your mouth properly. Speak properly.

But that is a schizophrenic sentence, and only of the ordinary sort. The "let's smoke a cigarette in Nantes at Christmas" sort. In Nantes, there is an exhibit. I go to the exhibit two years too late. In fact, there's an exhibition of the drawings of Lucio Fontana in the back room of the gallery, next to the empty fountain, which figures. A fountain is a portal. A fountain is regret. I look at each print, waiting for the diagonal mark on the page, but it doesn't come. Stupid me. I'm like a person waiting next to a fountain that's under construction for a lover who arrives, but is stupid. Is stupid to why we're here, meeting after all these years in a country that's full of white people all at once, irregardless of the suburbs. Do you come from a suburb? I come from a ditch.

I wrote schizophrenic sentence after schizophrenic sentence until I reached the last sentence, both after and before.

I wrote on a map littered with silver triangles and citron-yellow squares, which was not convenient but it was better than not writing anything at all.

Nevertheless, someone ought to take that map away from the cartographer and feed him some breakfast instead. He's so thin. He's so ill-looking. Give him some eggs. Give him some cold juice.

I want some juice, but I'm not so lucky. The store's all out. Back at home, tired out from the walk in the snow, I am writing about disease processes about fifty years too late; in fact, I wish I had been born in 1958 not 1968. At least then I would have existed as a figure in an epic narrative. As it is, I hold the book open with the heel of my left fist and write with the other, gripping the pen like an animal. At this late stage, I'm writing about a person's attempt to maintain a level of psychic intensity at all costs.

Another bad line.

Somebody give her a cup to drink out of. Somebody give her a bowl.

Hospital images are psychotic images. They bring forward the simple memories but the memories turn out to be tents. The pale pink membrane tears to reveal a full-grown man standing on a porch with his shirt unbuttoned, the fabric billowing in the breeze. He's super angry. He's quick to take her arm, to catch her hand.

18. *Race drops for Ban*

As a teenager, I was a Kundera fan. I analyzed his novels and saw that each of his first and third chapters opened with a gesture: the head turned over the left shoulder as the doctor walks past the swimming pool; the woman raising her arm to touch the rigid brim of her bowler hat in the oval mirror. And so on.

Feral events cut through.

That is why I am obsessed by them. They traverse public histories in a single line. They chart what remains undomesticated not as problems, but desires. How did the virus enter the human bloodstream for the first time? That's not desire, that's eating. That's eating something or touching something with eczematous skin.

Subtle race pride—eye-rolling when the woman in the fuchsia pink and chocolate silk sari entered the Wimpy Bar—and so on, was found to be a trigger for schizophrenia that far exceeded the actual stressor of migration.

We knew that in our bones yet when we found Butch and Sarah, two bedraggled English girls—one thin and one fat—abandoned beneath a bush next to the Churchfield Gardens, we took them home. My mum fed them curried okra and rice, with yoghurt and lime pickle, and later, toast. Nobody came to look for them, and they themselves could not recall being parented or even what lay beyond that field. It was getting late, so my mum gave them a towel to wash their faces and hands with. When they were clean, we showed them to a makeshift bed beneath the dining room table. But in the morning they were gone. They were cute.

A door you can't go back through.

As the event unfolds both after and before. As the text of a present moves so rapidly it cannot be written. This is why immigrants don't write many novels; only emigrants do. I write to you at night, for example, when even my body is hidden from view.

19. *London*

Radical modernity requires something of me.

An aesthetics of violence.

To write the larger scene.

In this scene without depth, rust-colored dust bleaches to a dirty white, like the urea of city birds that then drains off.

"Never hit a black woman." Elizabeth Lozano.

I tilt the paper to the left until all I can see are the clouds, blue and thick—though darkening—in the April sky.

She ate the sky.

The one thing that I can say about this awful night is that there are no possessions. There is nothing to buy or sell.

20. Regression for Ban

I am writing these words in a forest on the outskirts of Delhi. A crumbling pink wall, the ruin of a Mughal fort, extends to the horizon. My uncle says: "They were Eastern Europeans." I have a brief fantasy of a Prague café culture deep in the forest but when I look left there is just a blur of peacocks. The hologram of a peacock, that is, filled in by an emaciated sub-pink form. "Ghost zoo." Where am I? The heaps of scrap materials and organic matter are weirdly geometric. As always I extend my life by trying to be a person in India. Here a person might BECOME not just through acts of descent or alliance (to read India through Grosz) but through the volume and scope of matter itself. I watch the gold and creamy earth at the peak of its seasonal death turn into forms that keep moving, ebb then open up. This third form of becoming happens at the level of matter in India. The earth and the heat dominate personality. There is no Bergson here. I am writing these words on a Swedish keyboard: ääöööööåäö.

Driving through the forest at 4 a.m., I see small groups of well-dressed people on a vigorous walk. Some of them are housewives, their dupattas knotted behind their backs or off to the side so the arms can swing free. They are wearing printed cotton, asymmetrical batiks. Some of them are carrying long sticks, as are the young men who jog past the women in their immaculate sporting outfits: white vests and shorts, the occasional Puma tracksuit. I ask the taxi driver what's going on. He says: "Madam, they are BJP." BJP—the Hindu nationalist movement and party. "They are going to the stadium." They are striding and running to a stadium built for the recent Commonwealth Games. There, says the taxi driver, in excellent English, they sing the National Anthem and other patriotic songs aloud, followed by several rounds of calisthenics. Why the sticks?

"They are on patrol, madam."

It's time to go home.

I analyze my glimpse of the asphalt.

Many hours later, I open the window and below me, inches away, is Greenland. I see white mountains slashed with black vertical marks. I try to connect with Greenland. I place one palm on my chest and the other on the chest of Greenland, ignoring the plastic barrier between us, the sky.

21. *Embryology for Ban*

I clutch my notebook beneath my clothes. Beneath the street, an albino boa pushes its nose against the cement. The pavement tilts; the rain and blood slide off. A copper penny, iron alloys, fungus scraped from the crease of an ivy leaf by a fingernail. A black long hair slides off and is carried to Yeading High Street on the sole of a shoe.

Pink lightning fills the borough like a graph. I index the bandages and chunks of race passion to Ban.

Ban is a spine. Sometimes, looking at the watercolor drawing of an animal skeleton, I think her movements, even in the dying process, the spasms before death, are transforming her forever into something new.

The notebook lets something die in order to arrive.

Bronze scales glittering on the underside of the wave.

My cell-phone is held together with duct tape. I call my best friend.

The image that precedes Ban is the strangely intrusive image of a drowned woman. At the last moment, she escapes her husband's pyre, contorting or lifting her body into the river. She leaps into the river, fully clothed, her body on fire. That rapid cooling creates a bronze figure. River dolphins carry her to the Bay of Bengal, where microscopic sea creatures nibble away at the burns. This image of a woman, face up, floating in the dark water, stays with me for years.

My friend calls from Los Angeles to tell me her dream. She dreams I am face up, balanced on stones in a river, fire running over the top of my body. I save her voicemail until my phone breaks. She says: "What's going on?" Then one night, I have the following dream, the origin of the image I just described. Mid-ocean, a lightning storm fills the sky. A woman's body—inert, electrified—comes to life. Her eyes fly open. In the morning, I make a small drawing of a mermaid in my notebook and circle it with a maroon crayon.

Some bodies don't somatize.

Who they loved, where they went, what they were to another person.

They don't live.

There's no egg.

Uxbridge Road, London, 2012.

22. *London (2)*

I grew up three streets over from the Nestle factory, in a house with a larder.

Its bobbled window opened to the alley and whenever I visited my house, over the course of the next three decades, that glass was still there.

Tower blocks dominate the place I am from. Imagine a Parisian suburb.

If I can do this, if I can fictionalize the pack 'n' play, the patterned behavior of those early years, then I can do this. I can stand out in the rain.

Take your love back. You gave it to me. Now remove it. Cracked, flecked whiteness with deep blue folds. No more fats and sugars. No more bread or milk.

A girl lies down on the sidewalk. Tiny mirrors are balanced in the ivy next to her face. I never complete this work; instead, I keep balancing and tilting the mirrors. I travel to the U.K. and set a circular mirror in a nest of daffodils in Regent's Park, far from the street of the scene. Returning home, I lie down.

It is so excruciating to write about these subjects that I take years, months: to write them.

The many earth and sea layers make me sick.

I think about a monster to think about an immigrant, but Ban is neither of these things.

Service Road in front of Hotel 37, Mahipalpur (Airport) Flyover.
South Delhi, India, 2014.

23. *Mermaid Series for Ban: a contraction with enlarged font but no Kapil Muni*

It is the last day, and along the river, women are gathering the raw silk and cotton in coils of dripping color, feet bare, raw really and they're exhausted. This is the day that wires me to color but they are—most of the way through their own lives.

It is the last day I knew you in the time that we touched. And the more I write this, the more I realize how long ago it truly was that we touched. Centuries have passed and each life, I am born feet-first beneath a Lebanese cedar until finally, I am born in England on a summer's day, girls with pink ribbons in their hair trailing an even paler red light from their bodies as they gallop past on the street below. I count their cells. Each cell gives off a tiny bit of light. That light escapes; and yet, as the passage to rebirth narrows, I look away from them—fierce white animals that they are.

I knew you.

Come back.

Be mine.

I loved a man. A man with teeth made of channeled light—the white of lions. This is the language made available to me by English. Language does not survive death. I loved him and now—I search for him, scanning, at every airport and sometimes even in the supermarket in the large town to the north.

For more.

I can't sleep at night. Approaching death each time, I feel neither anxiety nor fear but relief that I can try again.

Come again.

It is the last day. It is 1895. It is 1431. It is 1972. We have been married for five months. I love him in a way that unknots me from the sky—from the inexorable flow of day into night. Even the day is night when he is near me. But he dies. He dies then dies again. We gasp—I gasp, my mother-in-law gasps—but die he does, in front of us, on the wet ground. We are in the courtyard when he buckles to his knees, then over to his side. He is walking to the kitchen from the bath, a threadbare towel thrown over his left shoulder, a thin cotton dhoti tied around his waist. July and so it's raining. Monsoon jasmine spilling out of our mouths when we scream: the air…

By nightfall, his pyre is prepared. A leaf wrapped around a mixture of nuts and a narcotic, an altering—powder—is pushed into my mouth. Drugged, I am propped between two others as I walk to the river pyre and there he is, there he is, there he is—a form.

Sheet, sticks, red powder and a fire—a fire is so cold…the red shape against the black river behind it, running hard. Monsoon…

And with a shove, and with a push.

I am gone.

No, they haven't lit it yet. I am lying on top of my husband. And when they set the fire, I don't feel anything.

Drugged.

Pretty.

Dressed in white.

The fire sobers me up. The fire reaches my foot and in that instant, terrifying everyone, I stand up. I stand up and I scream. I scream and I arch back. I arch back and I rotate. I twist in the air.

Imagine a woman leaping from a fire into the water.

For an instant, she's glimpsed—seen by others—face up—in that water, the fire running over the top of her body—and then swept—downstream—still ablaze.

The pink dolphins surge towards her. Why?

This is the last day.

Now my eyes are closed. The pink dolphins keep my mouth and nose above the water. Gradually, the calls of the men on the riverbank fade. I fall asleep. I fall into a deep sleep.

In this sleep, the dolphins carry me to the delta and then out to sea. There, a whale slips beneath and carries me farther in—deep into the true sea.

Tiny creatures come and nibble away at my burns—my legs and ankles fused together—until I am covered with coppery scars. My face a mask like a copper-colored leaf mixed now with a vertical skin, preserving it. My face. I drift beneath the falling stars, the blackness, the darkness, the river, for whom it is preserved.

And now I am dead. I am a mixture of dead and living things—all the creatures of the sea are breathing with me and for me, their mouths on my chin, my lips. The tiniest breathing of all. Their oxygen is like me. I am like them. For many hours I bob and select, with each breath, a continuing life but a storm is coming, the waves are crashing over my head—my head of long red hair, my white, creamy, and unreal skin—the pallor beneath the leaf—and even the whale needs to dive down now, renew his source of love.

And now, gradually at first and then with a great roar, mid-ocean: rain. A lightning bolt strikes me where I lie in my caul of throbbing weeds and fish. And this.

A next life.

My eyes flung open to the sky. To begin.

To live again—affixed to the circuitry of the non-living world. By nightfall, I was red.

Almost but never quite dead.

To begin. To never begin. To begin. To never begin. To begin. To never begin. To begin. To never begin. To begin. To never begin. To begin. To never begin. To begin. To never begin. To begin. To never begin. To beign.

Loveland, Colorado, 2012.

To bump.

To bump against land when I come to it.

To wash up. Why?

Yesterday, I oiled then braided my hair. I washed myself. I ate a balanced meal with milk. I poured a glass of milk into the sea.

Imagine the cloud of milk as it dissipates.

Now drink water.

I drink the water for Ban.

I write these notes for Ban.

You read these notes for Ban.

Why? I feel bad for you, having read this far into the nothing that these notes are.

And must be.

Neutral.

Stupid.

Bland.

Just as skin is bland and eases off the bones at the least touch.

Or tongue.

Of flame.

Venice Beach, Los Angeles, 2014.

END-NOTES

[Photograph, here, of Sharon Carlisle's garden/rectangle/clay installation in its final stages, dessicated and embedded with crystals? Or the mirror in the nest of daffodils in Regent's Park?]

I would like to thank the writers, artists and groups with whom I incubated the questions in *Ban*:

Sharon Carlisle: who dug a rectangle of earth in my back garden and let me lie in it, on the day between her preparation of the mud and the beginning of her own installation: the sculpture of a female Buddha in reclining pose. Like Sharon, I wanted to study what happens to bodies at the limit of their particular life. There was never a way to do this in writing. All summer, we analyzed the erosion and accretion of the blue chalk, shed leaves and patterned/humanized outline on the ground.

Sarah Roder: our conversations on embryology and cranio-sacral bodywork—how Ban's twitches and subtle movement were a form of discharge, an activity of the nervous system. Also: the art/earth experiments and mandalas we made, seasonally, next to the Big Thompson river in Colorado. The "unicorn chrysalis" we built/renewed in the garden every summer, weaving the elm tree's lower branches with red and turquoise wool. The bodywork language of imprint, fingertips, notochord, the watercolor map of the animal body, cellular migration and plant memory: is [are] hers.

Melissa Buzzeo: with whom I looked for unicorns in the Met and analyzed the body that is half-dead, half-alive. How the sea creature of *The Devastation* was profoundly in relation to Ban, stirring, somnolent, reptilian: a gesture-posture on the brink. Our meditations, book to book: sending energy [light] to the two books and the bodies in those books. Hers and Ban. A past-life regression that I once received—from Melissa—that opened the space of the butcher's shop: is also here. Performed. My spiritual goal as a writer was to break Ban's scene down; to make it rain so hard that the parts of her would flow. In fact, I could not accomplish this; Ban was a stain that kept blooming on the asphalt. The lightning did not accelerate decay; it did something else. Why doesn't Ban die off [become]? Melissa brought forward the discourse of waste material, abandonment, the "person left for dead" who—perversely—does not die. How to make (from this) (from these things): a form. A charnel: ground.

Andrew Wille: for encouraging me to write stories and to live a life of the imagination. On the day of the riot in 1979, I was safe beneath the blankets on the floor of my bedroom in Hayes. I made a novel from those muffled sounds. Then I wrote these, setting them aside: primitive stories set in the world that Ban is from, that I am from: a place and time that, in the manner of all urban ports, will not come again. A Punjabi enclave, thirty years on, is Sri Lankan and Romanian. I wanted to record a London that was never London, the place where Orwell lived—now long-gone. Andrew read these stories as they came, which was a gift. In the end, I deleted them and have stored them in another file—but for two years or more, they accompanied the fragments and perhaps that was what they were for. "To keep the world safe for poetry." –another A.W. Waldman, Anne.

My writing community at Naropa and Goddard: our work together on trauma, narrative, healing, poetry and the body. In particular, I would like to thank the students who participated in the Special Topics seminar: *Art is of the Animal*. We worked on embryology. We worked on the tectile, luminous parts of the brain that extend downwards into the body. Even the heart is formed through descent.

The Politics and Poetics cluster at UC Santa Cruz: for creating the conditions in which a sentence could be a butcher's shop; the commas orienting like hooks to a pre-historical space. The meat in the back room. How the semicolons denote pre-memory, carnage, deviation. The gift of the space the cluster offered me was immeasurable in approaching Ban as a pre-speech space: not linguistically, but in the sense of a body whose breath has been taken away.

Teresa Carmody and Amina Cain: for their curation of a Les Figues event: *Both Sides and Center*. For the gift of performing a "Schizophrene remix"—an alternate form of nudity—in a red sack in a window on a butcher's table, in the Schindler House in L.A. By compounding the voyeur section from *Schizophrene*, I was able—privately—to attend to the sensory details of an unwritten "Ban." To gather what you can never write: a witness account. To press against the red silk and visualize, in its entirety, a second and diurnal sun.

Bonny Taylor: for helping me to wire and light the Schindler House "butcher shop." For recording the knives and placing that recording in a bush outside the window. For dreaming of the river-Ban: water and fire mixed together on the front of the body, balanced on the stones. Shared consciousness. Sister. Friend.

Andrea Spain: for helping me to think about what a post-colonial literature might be. To write into the parts of institutions, societies and events that are never recorded or seen. Also: for helping me to critique the kind of vitalism I learned from Deleuze, Grosz and Haraway. How some bodies don't disseminate; they don't degrade. Are never washed away. This is the form of negation that I wanted to think about with Melissa, a negation that wasn't erased—as a way of marking, too, the violence received by the bodies of women in the place that I am [was] from. Andrea read a draft of Ban. She said: "Ban is a vector of refusal." Five minutes after talking to her on the phone, I got into my car and a piece of paper with the word "vector" in my own hand-writing flew off the dash that I had no memory of writing or placing: there. That summer, we performed a Masque for Ban at Naropa University's Summer Writing Program, choreographed by Andrea from Ban notes.

David Banash: for reading some of this in an earlier stage and encouraging me to write from the heart. See: Andrew Wille. I feel as if, when Ban is published, that I will sit down and a thousand stories will pour out.

Will Bemis: for building the writing hut. I cannot say I wrote Ban in the hut. I channeled Kapil Muni in the hut. As I did on Venice Beach. For Ban.

Kam Bhui: for inviting me to speak about these subjects at the World Conference of Cultural Psychiatry: London, 2012. The work with schizophrenia and migration—the studies of *Schizophrene*—precedes the work of Ban. A document, I wrote, of place. In London, I attended seminars on the riot, race factors and hallucination. I began to think about exposure and resilience: the parts of Ban that thrive, refract and make their own imagination. How do you interrupt top-down processing? To what degree are creative acts antidotes to the desire for cultural or institutional revenge?

Rohini and Asha Kapil, my sister and mother: who created their own art forms [visions] [lives] in a parallel space. Together, we made mandalas, drank chai and tried to make a life for ourselves as a family in the U.S. Who were we? The Brontës?

Thelonious, my son: for helping me to figure out how to catch or stop an orbital of soot. "You put a glass plate in the road, mom." He was correct. You have to set a trap. That was when I saw the nude page in my mind. And then the smudge.

Eleni Stecopoulos and Petra Kuppers: for creating community around healing, somatics and movement; in the Bay Area's *Poetics of Healing* series and in Michigan, at the *Writing, Movement, Somatics* research symposium.

Chris Chen, Dolores Dorantes and Jackie Wang: for making a frame. In their own particular language. For Ban. As per: the peach color that Margaret Tedesco selected for the cover, which references the ghost of the book, who was real: Blair Peach. Thank you to Margaret and also Stephen Motika for helping the material to settle on the page: a sedimentary tectonics. A simple design.

A Room of Her Own Foundation: for allowing me to teach through poetry and clay; the phenomenology of the female (mud) body that dissolves when it rains. In particular, I would like to thank the small groups of women who made *dushu* (devotional sculptures) with me at Ghost Ranch in 2011 and 2013.

The editors and journals who published early forms of BAN: nude smudges et al. Thank you Amy King, Ana Božičević and Kate Zambreno, in particular, for your encouragement of a notebook form. My apologies. I feel like I'm forgetting someone. The Asian American Writer's Workshop. Temple University's *Tinge. Black Warrior Review.* 1913? *Fact-Simile Trading Cards.* No. This is horrible. I am still not remembering some amazing place that published my writing. I truly apologize in advance. I don't know why I am not a normal person. Why didn't I keep track of these things? *English Language Notes. Bombay Gin. HTMLGIANT. BOMBlog. Everyday Genius. The Ancients. Moonroot.* Most recently, New Herring Press for publishing *TREINTE BAN: a psychiatric handbook for a work undone.* (A chapbook dedicated to Jackie Wang and Debbie Hu, who has since changed her name to Coda.) *Jacket 2.* The interview with Laynie Browne on the poet's novel. *Capilanou Review. Where Eagles Dare: East Bay Poetry Summit Edition.* Belladonna* Cooperative: for publishing *(a poem-essay, or precursor: NOTES: for a novel: Ban en Banlieues).*

Thank you to Anna Joy Springer and Amina Cain: for inviting me to speak about narrative and titration at the San Diego *And Now* and to Jena Osman for the week at Temple where I got to think through pilgrimage—recombinant fragments and ritual—for Ban. With gratitude, as well, to Samuel Delany for analyzing the problem of the chrysalis and resolving it in about two seconds, over a sloppy lunch of cafeteria meat. He said: "The chrysalis breaks off to form the wings."

Michelle Ellsworth: for her species/performance class at Naropa's Summer Writing Program, in which I graphed Ban's twitches to an index of clockwise and anti-clockwise movements as per Elizabeth Grosz's *Becoming Undone*. The language of the species as unregistered or not described came from her.

Thank you to Laura Mullen: for taking me to the edge of Louisiana, where we held sea creatures' pelvises over our faces like masks. Root-teacher. Friend.

With gratitude to Claudia Rankine for *Stories of Brown Girlhood*. Those stories, exchanged back and forth following our only meeting, activated the soul grief or autobiography that Ban also is.

Thank you to Mandeep Pannu: my life coach, who helped me to compile these fragments and orient to them in a timely manner, as she did with *Schizophrene*. If you are reading this and you also can't write or complete your book (or project of any kind), contact me and I will put you in touch with her IMMEDIATELY.

Thank you to my family in London, the Kingsbury Sharmas: who schlepped me to Hayes to lie down outside Grange Park school; to Arushi, in particular, for lying down next to the ivy, at the age of nine.

Thank you to Laura Campbell: for our conversations about Somatic Experiencing and the treatment of sexual/physical assault, a therapeutic frame I entrained to Ban: shaking, articulating herself (Ban) as a body, voltage: an animal: until she was done. I was interested in the nervous system: the way that bodies regulate aggression.

With gratitude to Suzanne Stein and the San Francisco Museum of Modern Art: for letting me incubate micro-movements and also Ban herself in the Gertrude Stein exhibit—posturing/twitching beneath the blue, geometric nudes. It is strange to think that this museum, as it was, no longer exists.

Thank you to Kelsey Street Press, Nightboat and Leon Works: for publishing my work on the immigrant, the monster, the schizophrenic and the wolf: concepts and figures that were precursors to Ban. Thank you, in particular, to Hazel White and Amber DiPietra, writers of the body and landscape in their own right. I think of Amber in her own performance at SFMOMA: lying down on the floor, enacting jellyfish consciousness: the bursting micro-movements of the disabled body—its scar tissue boundaries, its "you."

Thank you Erin Morrill: for looking after me in Oakland and helping me to be less rigid and boring than I usually am. We went to the part of the Californian coast where the earth broke off; glancing over, I saw Erin arcing up and back on a dune, like a sea-cobra of some kind.

Thank you to Juliana Spahr: for reminding me that beauty, magic and friendship are always possible when we open to them, in the company of others. With Jena Osman, she published my early work on cyborgs in *Chain*, the first writing of mine that appeared in a U.S. magazine.

Thank you to Thom Donovan: for helping me to understand that I was writing an "intense autobiography." Yes, my childhood nickname was BAN. John Bloomberg-Rissman, whom I have never met, wrote on this for *Galatea Resurrects*—and sent me books by

European authors in the mail. These books served as models— for the other kind of book that this could be. At the same time, I recalled—the oral-epic (mutated) Hindu forms—and tried to— stay close to those.

Thank you to Laynie Browne: for her kindness, tenderness and partnership near and for the healing narrative. What the poet's novel could be.

Thank you to Lisa Birman and Max Regan for holding the space with such love, always. And for their own imaginaries and forms.

Thank you to the readers of my blog, *Was Jack Kerouac A Punjabi?* I incubated Ban under your gaze. In a public notebook. Thank you for reading. I was writing for you. You know the truth. You know that I am not really a writer. You know that putting Ban in this form is like wearing a three piece suit in the hot springs. I wish I had the courage to let the blog be my book instead. Thank you for witnessing my life as a writer and, in particular, what it meant to write Ban.

Thank you to Kate Zambreno and [La Genet], Melissa Buzzeo, Gabrielle Civil, and David Buuck for performing works and rituals at the inaugural symposium (Violence and Community) at the *Jack Kerouac School of Disembodied Poetics*. The rotating fuschia pupae hung from hooks outside the administration building, the tent over the head, the prostrate body on the lawn outside the library, the group that was not allowed to resolve itself as a group: were images and scenes that broke the bounds of an academic setting. I felt attenuated. I felt like the person who could write Ban.

Thank you Rowland Saifi: for asking me the question: "What is Ban?" I began to answer his question and in doing so came to my politics. How does the Far Right organize and come to be, in a post-war society (1965–1983). And how do you track a parallel rise in ethnic (British Asian) fundamentalism within a citizenry? Ban is a set of pre-conditions, the most basic of premonitions, and so perhaps I also want to say that this feels linked: to the domestic (gender) violence, alcoholism and sexual abuse that unfold at home. Perhaps this is too massive a claim to make in a set of end-notes, but I am not sure where else to record it. Ban is historical fiction, in this sense. A book that I read during the early stages of Ban, that helped me to understand the cultural goals that I had as a writer, the desire to speak to the resurgence of anti-immigrant sentiment in Europe and a parallel organization of the Far Right, was Kurdo Baksi's *Steig Larsson: Our Days in Stockholm: A Memoir of a Friendship.* Once again, I don't know if I succeed in these goals in the book I have written; perhaps this is something I can work out in the next book, a novel not yet written—the rough ground where unicorns roam.

On that note, I would like to thank the painter Luke Butler: for giving me the ultra-long paintbrush that I wore to the Stein exhibit. It was a unicorn horn. I used it to gore Matisse. For Ban.

Thank you to Laura Ann Samuelson and Emily Harrison for a conversation about performance art and writing that feels like it has only just begun. It is an afternoon incubating future work with Laura Ann in a dance studio at Naropa University—hers and mine—that now opens this book! I accomplished more in 5 minutes with Laura Ann than I had in the 5 months before.

Schindler House, Los Angeles, 2011.

Thank you to Brook Houglam for inviting me to Vancouver to speak about Ban. I remember a conversation with Gail Scott about the image of ice falling through the trees. I remember Sina Queryas taking me to sit on a bench. I remember writing in the corridor with the workshop participants when we were locked out of the Kootenay School.

Thank you to the Bothell forest group for inviting me to speak to their community about hybrid biologies, a conversation about animals and monsters that underlies these notes.

Thank you to the other panelists at the insane *What are you projecting?* panel at the Seattle AWP. Crushing that charcoal I felt like myself; Ronaldo Wilson's PINK that followed felt, as I said, like the lightning I had been—longing for—so intensely.

With gratitude to CAConrad for the gift of a crystal: peacock ore.

Thank you to the Pratt Institute group that let me extend an idea of gendered time, activism and performance to the Fearless One: the moment that the book you are writing—begins to appear beyond itself. And to the Rose Garden, where I performed Ban—on all fours.

Thank you to Gingger Shankar, whose double violin was an analog to the animal or alien Ban I could not write. Vibration. Music. Molecules. The body disseminating into the night air of California, of all the places in the world. With gratitude to Neelanjana Bannerjee and Sunyoung Lee for their curation of Mehfil Massive and for the gift of collaborating with Gingger herself. I promised myself—on

April 23rd, 2014—that this would be the last time I would read from Ban. That it was time to finish Ban. As Gingger played *Dawn*, I stopped. On the aeroplane back to Colorado and now, tonight, I found a way to stop.

○○○○

Notes: The first piece I wrote for Ban was the section now called "Five Fictions for Ban." The idea of a woman whose work or art is retrospectively savaged by an art critic was the novel I wanted to write. I began to write images and scenes of another person's childhood that then became Ban. The artist's productions were feminist earth-works. In 2007, I drove to Des Moines to see a retrospective of Ana Mendieta's work and was haunted by the charred symbols on bark, *La Jungla*, the public work she was doing at the time of her death at 37. In other early versions of the novel, Ban's death is the catalyst for the riot; but when I asked who killed her—so many faces (both brown and white) came forward. Everybody did. Also, I did not want to contract or displace the death of Blair Peach, who was neither a petroleuse nor a participant in [of] a riot. He was protesting against the anti-immigrant policies of the National Front. It was a protest not a riot—in its early stage. I wanted to think, also, about Mendieta's work beyond the silueta—the street scenes with the blood sliding down and off the step. These were my aims.

For A Novel: I was interested in vibration. I was interested in what happens when you don't say anything at all. I wanted to open my mouth in a novel. I wanted to lie down forever in a novel. I dragged myself off the floor of the novel. I wanted to channel light to the mermaid drifting past Kapil Muni in the Bay of Bengal in a novel. Kapil Muni is my ancestor. Many centuries ago, he sat on a spit or island of sand. He does not appear in a physical form in Ban, though he helped what happens in Ban. Pink lightning. The rain. Peacock-copper wire. Circuits of light and color: of different kinds. I could not write this section at all, but began to channel Kapil Muni in another way—writing illegible texts for my friends and others who asked. Even this became overwhelming at times and I would stop. I feel ashamed that I could not make Ban an amazing book. I feel grateful that Kapil Muni came anyway, as the color and light that a novel contains. I transmit this light: to you. Can you feel it? I am sending it right now!!!!

Never written: In 2009, a man with a machine gun met me in the lobby of the Berkeley National Laboratory. I had made a prior appointment to meet Dr. John Dueber, an innovator in the field of metagenomics, to ask him for a definition of hybridity. He laughed. "An organism that shares a membrane with other organisms is a false indicator of hybrid form," I wrote afterwards, laboriously, so as not to forget, in the lobby, waiting for my ride. You can be hybrid and not share a body with anything else. Thus, the different parts of "Ban" do not touch. They never touch at all.

BUTCHER'S BLOCK APPENDIX

I wrote Ban in a sequence of notebooks that I transferred to a butcher's block in advance of these: "Notes."

[Photograph of Butcher's Block/Notebooks?]

Since 2009, when I started this book, I accumulated many notebooks. I cannot externalize [read them.] The butcher's block is not a static object in the red, gold and orange alcove in my home. On December 21st, 2012: having completed Ban: I will read the notebooks all at once and then not at all [again.] To open each notebook at random and write a sentence down: like a nerve or tendon—extracted, still living, for a few moments: in the air. Some of the notebooks got stuffed in from other times, and so I will include them too [rogue notebooks]. The notebooks are in the wire cages. I will select them as they come. This is bibliomancy: a form of divination that happens in a library space. New idea: I will stop when I get to Notebook 33. Thirty-three years since 1979: the year of the riot, Blair Peach's death: [Ban]:

Notebook 1 [6/17/07] [Rogue Notebook]:

"We asked you to describe a triptych, to write a definition for the magical dictionary. You said a triptych was continuous yet demarcated; that the break is built in. I am thinking of the gold peeling crust on the hinges between the icons: three wooden panels that fold into a box or open. Is a crucifixion a story or event, radiating its intensity across time? How will you adhere or join the three panels? Perhaps, for you, it will be a rotation, or simply the feeling that something is happening beyond our control—a mouth of blood dragged through each dark day."

Notebook 2 [12/30/10]:

"What do we share? We share a capacity for 'antagonism.' Aggressors die. Victims die. The matrix is not relational. It's not between them. It's vertical. It's the force that takes both of them down."

Notebook 3 [11/18/11]:

"I keep seeing the image Lars Von Trier has already incubated— an Ophelia drifting, caught in the weeds but also—streaming lightning from her hands; how the sister, Claire, comes upon Justine naked in the grove exposed to the planet Melancholia. How her husband takes the pills."

Notebook 4 [4/29/11]:

"For example, I met a man and lay down with him on a verge, repeating the race riot scene but in a context so far removed from its origin that it read, in its basic form, as shame. I made a verge or hill or rim out of everything. I made a woodland out of my life. I lay down beneath the trees in my life."

Notebook 5 [2/3/12]:

"To write an alter-ivy. To perform the novel. By lying down next to the ivy: exp./impl. Both open to the elements and of them, the surface dirt that packs the grooves of other people's shoes. The immigrant from Brazil is shot by a British police officer one evening and even this news turns into a kind of dirt. To write about England far from England. To approach Englishness as the thing that decays and to have watched it decay. 'You're not really English, though, are you?' said the poet. I felt ashamed."

Notebook 6 [4/2/07] [Rogue Notebook]:

"I wrote the convergent image, the one that exists in two places at once, and then I was done."

Notebook 7 [2/19/07] [Rogue Notebook]:

"The figure of the double proposes the life a figure can't continue. This is the figure reborn in a different time or even, in a pathological sense, the child. In another sense, the double is grotesque: an empty or void outline that drains the life of a dormant or helpless figure, in order to sustain that outline."

Notebook 8 [8/29/09]:

"What is the sexual story I came here to tell?"

Notebook 9 [7/6/04] [Rogue Notebook]:

"Narrative is kept secret and activated by certain words."

Notebook 10 [3/20/11]:

"I think, too, of Elizabeth Grosz's formulation of the fragment as "rough"—where the edge of it is, like glass or fur or light, so that it adheres to other fragments, not through historical or phatic means: but through the force of attraction. I place the fragments in a chrysalis: to recombine."

Notebook 11 [2/1/08] [Rogue Notebook]:

"Strata. Orbital."

Notebook 12 [12/31/09]:

"The sentence as the site of expropriation. A ritual of release. Texture. Let it begin with me. Basket, sense, fugitive. Notes, waiting for a 'crown.' Qualities displaced by a customer, customers asking for more: fur, content, ritual. Waiting for a 'crown' in a room. I was a bitch today."

Notebook 13 [7/17/08] [Rogue Notebook]:

"Fire. Milk. Red threads. Water. Green leaves from local bushes. Marigolds. Honey. Curd. Flowers—marigolds, tiny red roses. Rice grains. Poured again and again over the cobra [stone]. Symbols of the entity [Shiva]. Touching them then touching one's own forehead, eyes, throat, heart. Early morning in the temple. Dazzled to see all the elements I gather for Ana, that Ana gathered: here."

Notebook 14 [7/22/11]:

"A telegraphic English. A topical, alienated English. Regional English. A cosmology of English in which the verbs rotate on the tongue then drop onto the floor. Like rhythms. Like a speech that can't be sustained by the nerves. Frightening English. The English that gets through. Unlike archaic English. A fundamental address. And thus a text. A culminating, enduring text."

Notebook 15: [1/15/11]:

"For next week's class, please read: page 18: b52cb: Public Space. Wolf Prix writes: 'The empty space sandwiched between the two levels is the urban environment.' So, for writing practice: that would be: the identification of an 'empty space.' But one that's 'between.'"

Notebook 16: [7/22/11]:

"I write in a field of rye. I watch a woman let her hair down in a lit window. I blank out over my children's tea. I feel something. Love is posture. Aperture. Stance. I return to Town Beach. I slide onto the ground. I pin up my blonde hair and button up my grey coat."

Notebook 17: [4/25/10]:

"I made her a 'heart' from the red clay and maroon glitter; the shed blossomy husk bits as the cells and ridges of fat. An anatomy book open to get the valves right. Somehow giving up on the kitchen table to do this on the floor was right. A teapot of the Kuki-cha Brenda gave me as a gift. I made bodies of the dark pods—'spiky, soft'—and wet clay. Figures. Slogans. An atomic knot."

Notebook 18: [8/19/11]:

"Tarmac, D.I.A. Departing for Los Angeles. To be: both the meat and the butcher. To render: a symbolic scene. To render: a scene already looped—the thick gels, animal tags on the kitchen counter. This is flight, pitted. Dark green and silver metals are folded all around me. In my body are organs. Next, I think of Brian: fistula, abscess, a collapsed lung."

Notebook 19: [2/3/11]:

"Darker above, browner on the flanks. Wren-like, twitching, gleaming, inquisitive. The sequence is about not looking away."

Notebook 20: [2/23/11]:

"There's a word in embryology that already means the sentence. —J'Lyn Chapman."

Notebook 21: [11/7/07] [Rogue Notebook]:

"I think of the matrix of cloud, electrical light and ice—the land mass and atmosphere of England beneath this aeroplane. How, in the grid system, there are places still lit up. What is the convention of Indian writing in English? I keep drawing the horizon. The pink smear of a sun. The sunlight both a position: and an entity. Disc-like. Yet static. It's time to get on."

Notebook 22: [6/10/11]:

"This week I taught a class on the category of prose. I said that prose was not social LIFE in the way that novels are: documents: of worlds. 'Worlding.' —Haraway. I want to write the worlds that vanish almost as soon as they are made. Legal and illegal: arrival. Crossing. But also an academic or bourgeois diaspora: too: how the radical sexual choices, the ones that got you out of London, are also the ones that don't allow you to return."

Notebook 23: [1/18/04] [Rogue Notebook]:

"Blackening the pages is writing. Circuitry. Detach the arms from the legs and rub dry with 'silver mittens.'"

Notebook 24: [9/30/09]:

"What is a vengeful point of view? How did Ban die? Describe Ban's hair. Eat as Ban would eat. Who leaves Ban? What is Ban's oblivion? Ban is a lovely adventurer who has left it too late in life to find love exactly. I write that and see Ban. Walking to Pinner Station. Ban's dead. Ban's eyes are light brown like a boy's. Ban is more beautiful than you. Ban shines. Ban beneath Minerva's Bell. Ban in Starbucks. Ban's parents? Ban's people? Ban's earth? Ban's flight? What is Ban's favorite film? Ban arcs, hits a membrane, then flips again: aphasic, she gathers her energy to arc again."

Notebook 25 [11/11/06] [Rogue Notebook]:

"Melissa, café. This unrecorded life. Small ecosystems where we don't see what's being destroyed or what's emerging. Acts that don't reproduce. A question of uselessness. (Bataille.) Melissa brings the coffee and then the cream, in a little jar."

Notebook 26 [10/4/09]:

"Style/grammar: notes. Technical architectures: polytunnels, an inverted tree, an elm woven with cloth strips, willow branches, metallic elements. A shelter. A method. A garden. A staunch definition: all meshed up. Ruined. I wanted to design a floating home, like the Kashmiri houses on stilts: windows with no glass, families wrapped in quilts on the floor."

Notebook 27 [1/2/08] [Rogue Notebook]:

"On the plane above Kabul. Thelonious brought a red balloon. Above Afghanistan. He's sleeping now. En route to India, I'm out of touch. In this sky with my son. Post-genre. Hybridity is a genre still forming. Hybridity is building something to attract not the insects: but the light. So, in a way, it's a void, a kind of fertility. Why don't I write?"

Notebook 28 [11/9/10]:

"Copper and dull gold—asphalt. I read the blogs of Ron Silliman, Kate Zambreno, Dodie Bellamy, Zadie Smith. You name it. I give my personhood to media outlets of all kinds. Plugging in to the wrong thing. The sun is there. I receive a galactic beam, casually. In a sacrifice, the light is received: by whom? The process of healing happens through: dormancy. Multiple occasions of healing—small acts of dignity, tenderness, kindness. Past life cycles: repetition, violence. What happens to the mermaid? Voltage, Ban. A slow, weird, ecstatic death. Ban."

Notebook 29 [8/28/10]:

"This is why I write: to unfold the electrical mat of my nervous system. The nerves all blue, red and yellow with flaring nodes. This is my cyborg text. It is planar. It is a substitute for other forms of speech, or intimacy. Glissant: 'nonhistory.' The boundaries of my work are 'structurally weak': Glissant. What weakened them? Violence. I could not bear to be touched. In adult life, I wept like a baby when the man I was with refused to get a divorce."

Notebook 30 [4/22/06] [Rogue Notebook]:

"What happens when a wave goes over a life?"

Notebook 31 [11/18/09]:

"Read a bit of Žižek to figure out: 1. Event/body. (9/11 'I love you' calls.) 2. One or two sentences: declarative, oppositional. (The turn.) 3. Several paragraphs with a sustained query/logic that is beautiful/compelling but also constitute (Z): A FALSE OR WIERDLY ILLOGICAL TURN."

Notebook 32 [11/9/12]:

"Darkness is a product of our own retina. —Anne W.
The contemporary is the one whose eyes are struck by the beams of darkness that come from his own time. —Agamben.
Ban: creature, vertebra/spine, waves, century, face."

Notebook 33 [10/9/11]:

"To write: again. The role of decomposition in the body's forming: becoming-mermaid. The role of sacrifice, patriarchy, fire-water mixtures. The notes at the back of the Penway composition book as the "bright salty" that precede this notebook's aims. I want to find out if I am a writer. To write chronicity, titration: the nerves. How it's not the event but what precedes [follows] it. Is this the mirror stage? Ask M. Write: the findings. Write what never ends."

Nightboat Books, a nonprofit organization, seeks to develop audiences for writers whose work resists convention and transcends boundaries. We publish books rich with poignancy, intelligence, and risk. Please visit our website, www.nightboat.org, to learn about our titles and how you can support our future publications.

The following individuals have supported the publication of this book. We thank them for their generosity and commitment to the mission of Nightboat Books:

Kazim Ali
Elizabeth Motika
Benjamin Taylor

In addition, this book has been made possible, in part, by a grant from the New York State Council on the Arts Literature Program.